I draw, I paint

colored pencils

Text: Isidro Sánchez
Drawings: Jordi Segú
Illustrations: Jordi Sábat

English translation © Copyright 1991 by Barron's Educational Series, Inc.

© Parramón Ediciones, S.A. 1991

The title of the Spanish edition is *Yo dibujo, yo pinto lápices de colores*

All inquiries should be addressed to:
Barron's Educational Series, Inc.
250 Wireless Boulevard
Hauppauge, New York 11788

Library of Congress Catalog Card No. 91-14932

International Standard Book No. 0-8120-4719-2

Library of Congress Cataloging-in-Publication Data

Sánchez, Isidro.
    [Yo dibujo, yo pinto lápices de colores.   English]
    Colored pencils: the materials, techniques, and exercises to teach
yourself to draw with colored pencils / by Isidro Sánchez ; drawings
by Jordi Segú ; illustrated by Jordi Sábat.
        p.   cm. — (I draw, I paint)
    Translation of: Yo dibujo, yo pinto lápices de colores.
    ISBN 0-8120-4719-2
    1. Colored pencils.   2. Colored pencil drawing — Technique.
I. Title.   II. Series.
NC892.S2613   1991   91-14932
741.2'4 — dc20   CIP

L.D.: B-7155-91
Printed in Spain
1234   987654321

I draw, I paint

colored pencils

The materials, techniques, and
exercises to teach yourself to draw with colored pencils

CHILDRENS PRESS CHOICE

A Barron's title selected for educational distribution

ISBN 0-516-08462-3

What are...

A pictorial technique

You undoubtedly made some of your first drawings with colored pencils. That is why you probably associate them with children's drawing.

However, the technique of colored pencils has been used by many great masters—especially the Impressionists. Today, this technique is used by painters, graphic artists, and advertising illustrators.

This book shows the materials and explains the technique of using colored pencils. As with all the titles in this series, it has been edited with the aim of teaching you the technique through progressively difficult exercises.

This book teaches you how to draw with colored pencils.

Practice the technique and carry out the exercises. You will certainly be able to create works such as the one you see on this page.

Drawing with colored pencils

The technique of drawing with colored pencils allows you to create your own works, which you will certainly be proud of.

Colored pencils are also a good way to prepare to use other techniques, such as watercolor, tempera, or gouache.

Without having to know how to use a brush, you can learn important lessons about painting, such as:

– Understanding color.
– How to lighten and darken colors.
– How to mix colors.

The pressure you exert on the pencil allows you to obtain different values: (1) a weak value by pressing lightly; a medium value by pressing a little harder, and a strong value by applying a lot of pressure to cover the grain of the paper. With colored pencils you will also learn: (2) to gradate and (3) to mix colors.

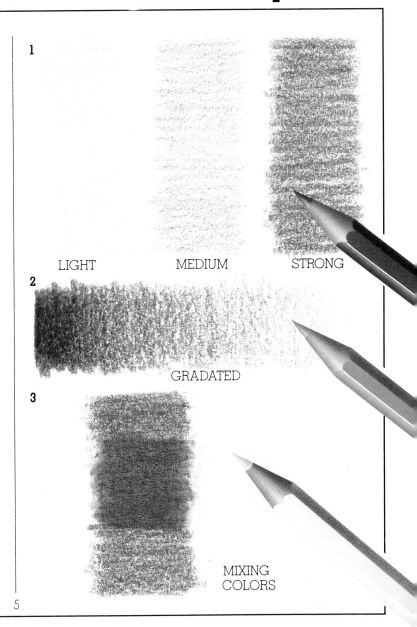

1

LIGHT   MEDIUM   STRONG

2

GRADATED

3

MIXING
COLORS

What I draw with...

How colored pencils are manufactured

The lead in colored pencils is made of pigments bound with wax and a type of clay called kaolin.

This is the essential difference between colored pencils and graphite pencils.

Graphite pencils have several different degrees of hardness, while colored pencils have just one degree, generally called either soft or semisoft.

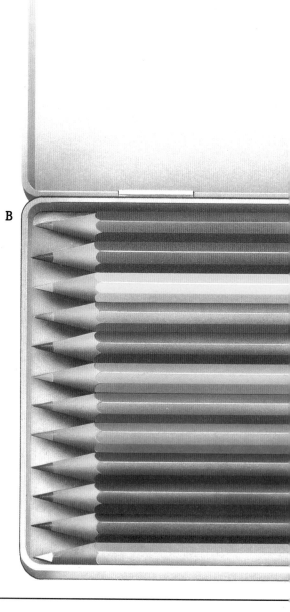

Graphite pencils—the ones next to these lines—have different degrees of hardness, from B or soft pencils, through HB or semisoft pencils, to H or hard pencils. This gradation doesn't exist for colored pencils, which usually are semisoft. To the right you can see a cross section of a colored pencil showing (A) the pigment lead in (B) a wood covering.

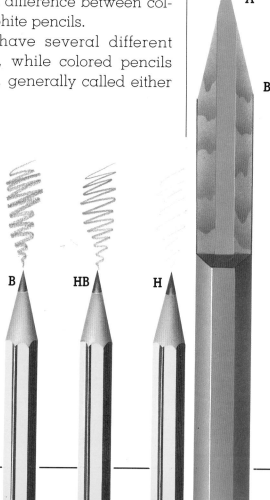

A 12-color box provides all the colors you need. In fact, you could work with only the three colors on the right—the primary colors, which we'll discuss later.

Nevertheless, in the beginning you should use the range of shades you have in your 12-color box in order to avoid mixing colors.

How many colors do you need?

There is a great variety of boxes of colored pencils. Sets are available containing 8, 12, 24, 36, 48, 60, and 72 colors.

If you use one of the larger sets, you will have a huge range of different shades. Some professionals use these assortments to avoid mixing colors, which may result in damage to the paper grain.

As a beginner, you need an assortment of only 12 colors, including:

Orange
Red
Yellow
Yellow ocher
Brown
Light green
Dark green
Light blue
Dark blue
Purple
Black
White

What I draw with...

What paper to use

The various types of paper are classified according to their weight and texture.

Weight is the paper's thickness measured in pounds. A paper that weighs 16 pounds is a thin paper, whereas a paper that weighs 140 pounds is a thick paper—almost a cardboard.

Texture is the greater or lesser roughness of the paper surface. It is also called paper grain.

There are three classes of texture: smooth (hot press), medium (cold press), and rough.

There are also glossy papers, with a shiny surface.

The best papers for use with colored pencils have a smooth or medium surface.

PAPER PAD

ROUGH PAPER

SMOOTH PAPER

MEDIUM PAPER

Colored paper

As you have just learned, various kinds of paper can be distinguished according to their weight and texture. But we can also choose between white and colored papers.

The choice between white and colored paper depends on the subject you are going to draw.

Usually, if you draw on colored paper, the color contributes to the "atmosphere" of the work you are drawing.

Art stores stock a wide range of tones.

On the right you can see the possibilities of working with colored paper. A paper in the color of the subject works as an extra background. There is a wide range of colors to choose from, but usually the most suitable are the neutral ones.

What I draw with...

Supplementary materials

All techniques require various supplementary materials.

Sharpening the pencil

Colored pencils have to be sharpened frequently. There are different ways of getting a point on a pencil. You need a pencil sharpener and sandpaper. With sandpaper you can make a very sharp point for fine lines and tiny details. Rub the point horizontally on the paper while turning the pencil.

CONTAINER FOR
THE PENCILS

A
B

To avoid the constant search for pencils, have them at hand in a jar. Keep them with the points up, the way you see them in the picture. Observe the difference between a pencil sharpened (A) with a knife and (B) with a pencil sharpener.

SHARPENER   SANDPAPER

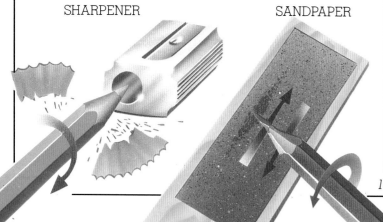

A container for the pencils

To spare yourself the constant search for pencils, keep them at hand in an earthenware, glass, or plastic jar. The most frequently-used pencils are stored there, always with the points up.

A wooden board

A sloping board is ideal for working comfortably. You can hold it on your knees and lean it against the table edge.

If you use a wooden board, try to get a spring clip like the one in the illustration to hold the paper to the board. You can also use thumbtacks.

Notebook for sketches and folder

You will need a notebook for making sketches in preparation for the final drawing.

Keep your work in a large folder. Place sheets of paper between the finished works.

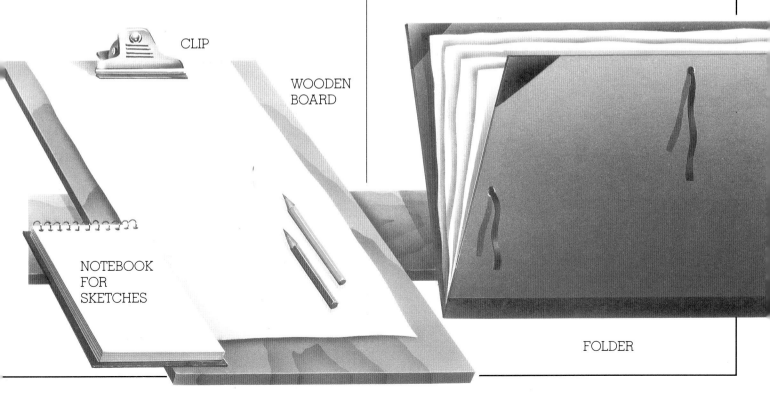

CLIP

WOODEN BOARD

NOTEBOOK FOR SKETCHES

FOLDER

How I draw...

How to hold the pencil

To draw with colored pencils, hold the pencil between the first two fingers and the thumb, as you normally grip it for writing. This is especially true when drawing details or small areas.

Usually, the pencil is held slanting slightly on the paper.

When you color a large gradated area, such as a background, it is better to hold the pencil almost horizontal to the paper, with the shaft in the hand.

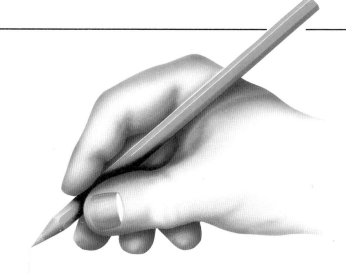

A. FINE LINES: HOLD THE PENCIL AS YOU DO WHEN WRITING

Here you can see two usual ways to hold the pencil. However, every artist does it in the most comfortable way for him or her to best direct the pencil.

For fine lines or details, hold the pencil as you do when writing (A). For gradations and large areas, many artists hold the pencil with the shaft in the hand and the point horizontal to the paper (B).

B. GRADATIONS AND LARGE AREAS: HOLD THE PENCIL WITH THE SHAFT IN THE HAND

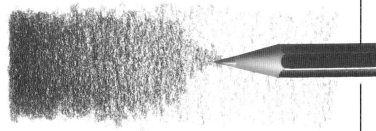

1. FIRST APPLY THE
LIGHTER COLOR

2. THEN SUPERIMPOSE
THE DARKER COLOR

Always color from less to more

To color from less to more means to first apply the lighter colors and then gradually superimpose the darker ones.

The lighter colors of the pencils do not cover the darker ones.

Always begin toning gently, using lighter colors and barely putting pressure on the pencil. Don't forget that the order in which you apply the colors is very important.

In this way, coloring from less to more, you can intensify tones and mix colors later by superimposing them, as you will see in the following pages.

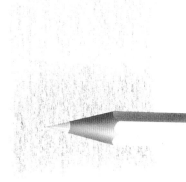

The order in which you apply the colors is very important both for mixing colors and obtaining tones and values. If you first apply yellow and then apply blue, you will get a dark green. However, if you apply blue first and then apply yellow, you will get a light green.

How I draw...

How to color

By exerting a different pressure on the paper, you will get lighter or darker tones.

You can see this as follows:

Color a wide area in red, pressing gently. The color will be very light, almost orange.

Then color, pressing hard. You will obtain a dark, intense red.

Take the paper grain into account

When drawing with colored pencils, the results obtained greatly depend on the paper grain.

If you press gently on the paper, the pigment will not cover the tiny protuberances. If you press hard, the white will be filled in.

Nevertheless, it is not practical to press too hard on the paper. You could destroy the paper grain, thus creating a smooth surface on which the pencil lead would slide.

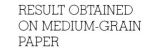
RESULT OBTAINED ON MEDIUM-GRAIN PAPER

Look at the tone obtained by pressing gently on the paper. On the right, a darker tone of the same color is obtained by pressing harder.

The choice of paper grain will affect the final result. When drawing with colored pencils, it is better to use fine- and medium-grain papers.

14

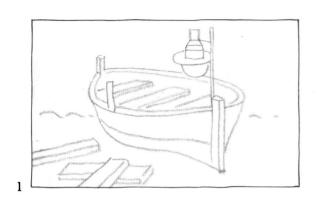

1

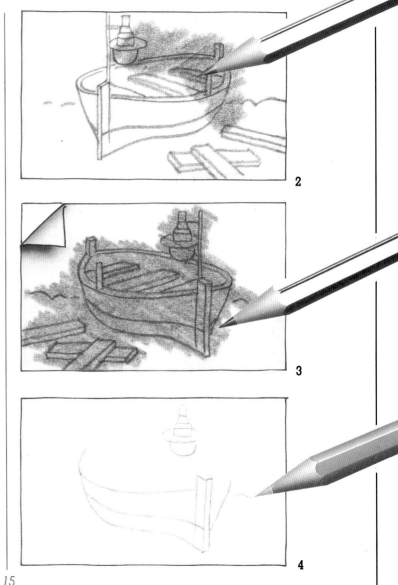

2

3

4

A very useful system

When working with colored pencils, the initial drawing should be made with a color harmonious with the main color of the work.

If you are hesitant about drawing with a colored pencil, the following method will solve the problem.

Draw with graphite pencil on tracing paper. You can erase what you don't like until you are satisfied with the drawing (1).

Smudge the back of the tracing paper with a soft pencil (2).

Place the tracing paper on the drawing paper, dark side down, and go over the drawing (3). Then, simply redraw it with a colored pencil (4).

How I draw...

How to make gradations

To make a gradation you must know how to achieve different tones of a color, from the darkest to the lightest.

It is not difficult but you must practice using the pencil with various pressures to obtain different tones.

Let's begin. First, take a red pencil and begin to gradate, pressing hard on the paper and then gradually reducing the pressure.

Keep your strokes rather short so that you can make a zigzag from top to bottom without stopping.

At the end, you will be scarcely brushing the surface of the paper.

In some places you will still have irregular tones or lighter tones. Retouch these with the utmost care, applying more or less pressure according to the area.

Begin by drawing a zigzag from top to bottom, pressing hard at first, then, little by little, more gently until the end, when you will be scarcely brushing the surface of the paper (1). Then, retouch those areas with irregular tones or lighter tones, pressing just enough, depending on where you are in the gradation (2). The final result should look like illustration 3.

1

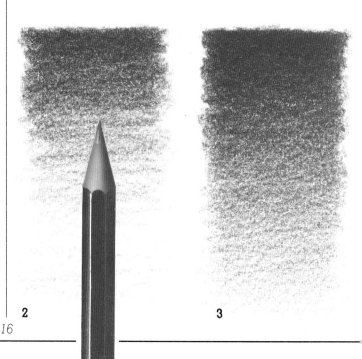

2

3

How to mix colors

Color mixing is obtained by superimposing colors on the paper surface.

The grain of the paper is very important in the mixing results.

As we have seen, when you draw gently on a fine- or medium-grain paper, tiny white areas are left.

If you apply a new layer to the same area you will cover more of the white paper that was showing through.

Superimposing two colors produces a new color by means of the *optical mix*, in the same way that a new tone is achieved by superimposing different layers of the same color.

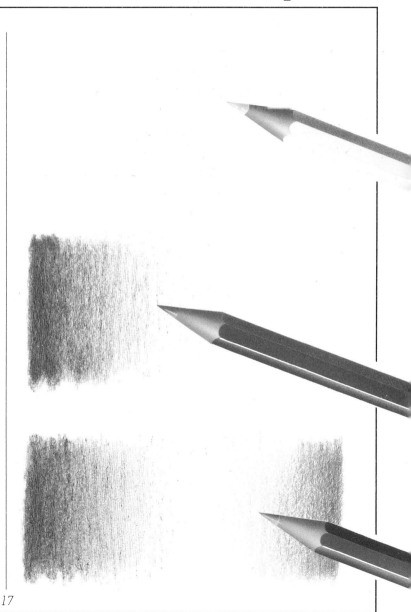

In this exercise on color mixing you will also practice gradations. Observe that when you apply red to a yellow background, the intense color at the beginning of the gradation changes to a lighter tone when you press gently on the paper. You have mixed yellow with red and have obtained different tones of orange. Similarly, you get a whole range of tones in green when you mix blue with yellow.

Color theory

The primary colors

There are three basic colors in your colored-pencil box.

They are the *primary colors*—blue, red, and yellow.

Mixing them in pairs, you get the so-called *secondary colors*—purple, orange, and green.

By mixing the primary colors and the secondary colors in pairs, you will obtain the *tertiary colors*, such as blue-violet, red-orange, etc.

MIXING
PRIMARY COLORS

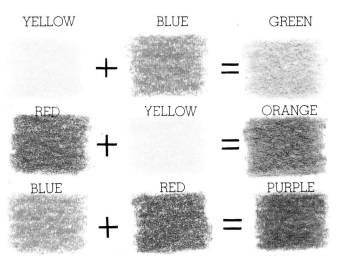

YELLOW + BLUE = GREEN

RED + YELLOW = ORANGE

BLUE + RED = PURPLE

All the colors

But you can also obtain all the colors by mixing just the three primary colors: blue, red, and yellow.

Practice mixing these three colors. Later you will have to use just these primary colors.

The color wheel

The color wheel consists of the three primary colors, the three secondary colors, and the six tertiary colors, making a chromatic circle of twelve colors.

In the chromatic circle you can see several arrows pointing to opposing colors. These are the *complementary colors*.

With the complementary colors you can obtain intense contrasts of color and many other possibilities that you will discover.

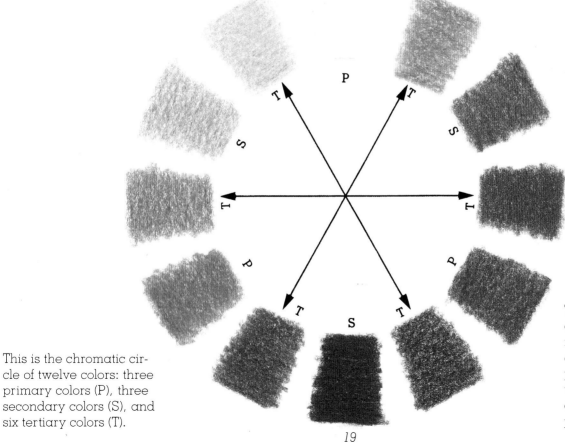

This is the chromatic circle of twelve colors: three primary colors (P), three secondary colors (S), and six tertiary colors (T).

The arrows relate the colors to their complementary colors. The *complementary colors* produce the most contrast. These contrasts offer many different possibilities to the artist.

My first exercises...

Draw the outlines of the balloon with a blue pencil, without pressing too hard. Draw the high-

light on each balloon. Fill in with color, holding the pencil horizontal to the paper. Press gently.

Draw the flower in great detail—all of the details will be helpful when coloring.

Using gentle pressure, color the flower petals a uniform light-yellow.

Use the same colored pencils to obtain darker tones for the shaded areas.

Retouch the shadows and gradate toward the lighter areas to obtain volume.

Repeat the same procedure, coloring the corolla, leaves, and stem in pink and light green.

Work on the shadows with dark yellow and pink and outline the contour of the flower.

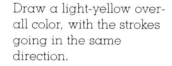

Make a line drawing, paying attention to the proportions, without indicating the shadows.

Draw a light-yellow over-all color, with the strokes going in the same direction.

In the next exercises, you will begin to practice gradations and color mixing.

Use pink and light green, gently pressing the pencil on the paper, to gradate the wing area.

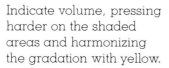

Shape the leaf with the strokes, pressing harder on the lower half.

Indicate volume, pressing harder on the shaded areas and harmonizing the gradation with yellow.

Color the rest. By means of the gradation, join the previous colors. Use purple for the eye.

Harmonize the different colors in the intermediate areas.

My first exercises...

Make as detailed a drawing as possible. The more details you have, the easier it will be for you to work exclusively with the color.

The first touches of color: Apply a light yellow background to the front and central stripes of the skateboard. Then, apply light green.

Color the ball and the remaining stripes of the skateboard. Intensify the stripes with dark green.

Darken the shadows. Show the volume of the ball by darkening the tones and gradating to the center. Work on the skateboard color. Color the wheels and use black on top of brown in the shadow areas.

In this exercise, you will practice outlining. Draw the aquarium outline, using a ruler if necessary.
You must keep your pencils sharpened, especially in

drawing exercises, such as this one. First, draw the contour of each element and then, fill them in with color.

Use light green for the aquarium bottom, always with the same strokes. Intensify all the tones, filling in one fish's fin with orange.

Pay special attention to the rendering of the water. Apply pressure to the pencil in some areas and then gradually reduce the pressure. Harmonize the color of all the fish while developing the shadows.

My first exercises...

In this exercise, as in the previous one, you will practice contouring and developing dark tones.

In the beginning of this exercise, you must pay attention to the large butterfly's wings. Observe the distinct width of the markings.

Color all the butterflies. Hold the pencil horizontal to the paper and make even strokes. Don't press the pencil too hard. You should achieve smooth tones that you will intensify later.

Harmonize each color. Then, apply the details on the butterflies' wings. Make strong strokes for the grass, using dark green on a light yellow background.

In this exercise, you will practice creating shadows and darkening tones. First, carefully draw the elements of the landscape.

Apply a first layer of color on the treetops, holding the pencil almost horizontal to the paper, and making all the strokes in the same direction.

Do the same with light green on the foreground. Use yellow for the first layer of the background. The tree trunks must have the same kind of strokes.

Work the shadows on the treetops with strong strokes. Make a gradation to the center of the tree trunks, especially in the nearest one.

My first exercises...

If you draw directly with the blue pencil, try not to press too hard. Use of the eraser should be restricted when drawing with colored pencils to avoid smudging the drawing.

Before beginning your next exercises with colored pencils, here are two points to keep in mind.
– Put a sheet of paper under your hand to avoid smudging the drawing.

– If you are hesitant about doing the drawing with a colored pencil, draw with a graphite pencil on tracing paper. Then, use the procedure explained on page 15 to copy it onto the drawing paper.

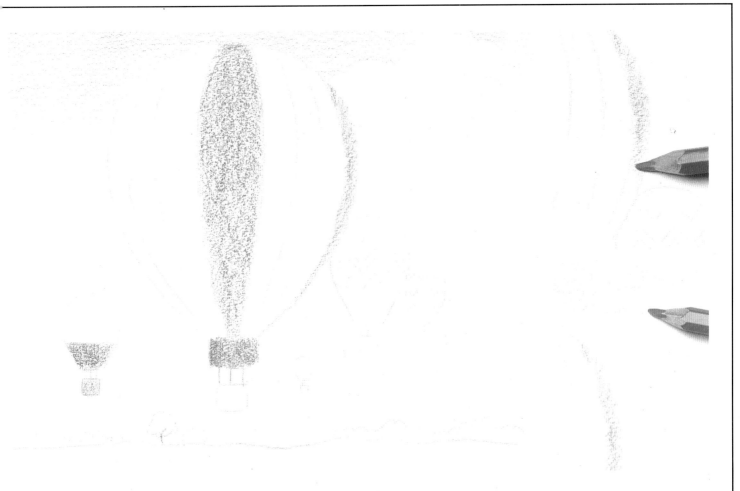

First, color the blue stripes. Use horizontal strokes from the top to the bottom. Then, intensify the tone, applying vertical strokes.

Draw the contours of the clouds. Then, begin coloring the sky from the top. Hold the pencil point horizontal to the paper and draw with horizontal strokes.

You should press harder in the beginning and reduce the pressure in the lower area.

My first exercises...

Color the yellow, red, and green stripes of the largest balloon with light strokes, without putting too much pressure on the pencil.

Also apply the first layers of color on the remaining balloons.

Try not to exceed the outline of the drawing, especially in the balloon on the right.

Apply more color to all the stripes to obtain stronger tones.

Hold the pencil almost horizontal to the paper and draw with long, sideways strokes to produce the yellow ocher area in the foreground.

Color the bushes with light green and then, reinforce them with some strokes in dark green.

Make long, sideways strokes with yellow ocher in the foreground; intensify the tone with yellow.

Use darker tones of each color to finish the balloon.

Finally, gradate the blue of the sky with white.

29

My first exercises...

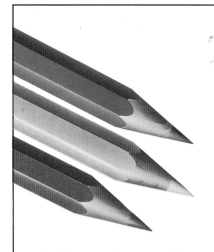

In this exercise, you will work with only three colors: blue, red, and yellow. You'll be surprised at the results.

As you have already seen, by mixing primary colors in pairs, you will obtain secondary colors. The mixture of the three primary colors results in black.

Wouldn't you like to practice these possibilities with the primary colors?

First use the red pencil.

Hold the pencil point horizontal to the paper and press on it lightly.

Press harder, going back over the darker areas.

Remember you should always color using the same stroke—in this exercise a straight, sideways stroke. For instance, notice that the stroke for the trunk always goes in the same direction.

My first exercises...

Now we add two other colors.

Add blue over the red for the shadow areas, applying pressure to the pencil.

Color a light layer on the treetop and the bushes.

Add yellow to the darkest area of the feathers and then, draw light strokes of yellow over the blue to obtain the green for the treetop and the bushes.

In this finishing stage, you obtain mixtures by superimposing and gradating one color over another. This is a way to harmonize the areas between the colors.

Add blue to the trunk and the treetop, pressing harder. Then, color with yellow to obtain an intense tone. Remember: blue, yellow, blue, yellow...

Draw the outline of the trunk with dark blue and, pressing harder, recolor the shadow areas, pressing more lightly toward the center.

Finally, add light strokes of blue to the bushes to obtain a darker green.

My first exercises...

This and the following exercise will improve your technique with colored pencils. You will practice color mixing and making tones. Don't forget:
– to take care that the strokes have the same direction and width.
– to begin with the light colors; you will intensify the tones progressively. If you had to erase large areas you would probably smudge the whole work. Be careful not to overdo the intensity of color.

Following the model, make a line drawing. Draw the contours of the shapes in the landscape, ignoring the areas of shadow.

Pay special attention to drawing the span of the bridge. The sides and the arch must be in the right perspective.

Use light yellow to color the grass in the foreground; don't press hard on the paper, and draw sideways strokes all in the same direction.

Apply the first layer of yellow to the treetop. Color the meadow light green and the shadows of the treetop dark green.

My first exercises...

Barely pressing the pencil on the paper, color with long, regular strokes for the meadows. Try not to exceed the lines of the bridge.

Begin coloring the sky in light blue. To gradate, use the technique you've already learned. Press the pencil harder on the upper area and just barely brush the paper on the lower area.

With the same blue, draw ripple strokes for the river. Press harder to convey the bridge shadow. Shape the trees in the background with loose strokes.

Color the trunk dark brown with regular strokes in the same direction.

Fill in the bridge front with light brown, using even pressure to obtain a uniform tone.

Do the same for the underside of the arch, pressing a bit harder.

Mix light brown into the bridge reflection in the water. Harmonize with very light blue.

My first exercises...

Color with irregular strokes, pressing the pencil harder on the paper to intensify the color in some areas of the river.

Use the red pencil to color the roof, barely pressing on the paper. Intensify the tone of the shadow under the eave.

Color the chimney.

Draw a red line to fix the limit of the river bank. Intensify the shadows with dark blue.

Now, create dark tones to achieve the feeling of volume.

Work with dark green, mainly on the lower right-hand area of the treetop. Draw strong strokes in the same direction as in the rest of the exercise.

Use dark brown on the trunk, with the most intense tones on the outer area gradating to the center.

My first exercises...

This drawing of a truck is
not difficult. However, if
you are uncertain about
doing this subject, use
a ruler.

Using either a blue or a graphite pencil, draw this picture, following the previous instructions for the technique.

Use a ruler to draw the truck.

Different systems, such as the use of a grid and tracing, are used by many artists for drawing.

Apply a first layer of color to the back of the truck (the trailer), holding the yellow pencil horizontal to the paper and drawing the outlines accurately.

Gradate with yellow ocher and light brown. Apply pressure for the area by the road and reduce the pressure gradually.

My first exercises...

Color the lower area of
the cab. Don't worry
about the lines of the
drawing. Draw the out-
line of the window in the
upper area.

Use red to color the cab. Don't be concerned if
you cover the blue lines. Color the design on the
trailer red.

Sharpen the orange pencil; you will need a
very sharp point to draw the exhaust pipe and
the upper part of the hood.

Now you will work only with blue. It will be very useful for practicing different tones of a color.

Gradate the sky with light blue and also use light blue for the reflections on the window glass, the tires, and the smoke.

Color the sides of the wheels with dark blue, especially the left front wheel.

43

My first exercises...

With strong strokes, using light green and holding the pencil horizontal to the paper, color the bushes in the foreground and background.

Apply a first layer of light brown to the road, pressing the pencil harder for the shadow of the truck. Use purple under the bumper and the back of the truck.

Harmonize the yellow background with vertical strokes in yellow ocher. Hold the pencil horizontal to the paper and press gently to avoid obvious strokes.

Without pressing hard on the paper, harmonize the color of the cab with vertical strokes of light brown.

Retouch and draw the outlines of the wheels in black, and use purple in the shadows.

Mix dark blue with the brown of the road.

Draw all the contours, with dark green for the bushes, dark blue for the horn and the bumper, and dark brown for the radiator grill and the exhaust pipe.

Glossary

chromatic circle. A circle made up of twelve colors: three primaries, three secondaries, and six tertiaries. Another name for chromatic circle is color wheel.

complementary colors. The secondary color obtained by mixing two primary colors is complementary to the third primary color (for example, green, obtained by mixing blue and yellow, is complementary to red).

composition. The arrangement of all elements of a subject in a pleasing way.

cool colors. Those that in the color wheel are located between green and violet, with both these colors included.

form sketch. Preliminary lines in a drawing that set down the basic forms of a subject by means of simple geometric shapes (squares, rectangles, circles, etc.).

gouache. A technique of painting in which watercolors are mixed with opaque white pigments causing colors to lose their transparency.

gradation. The gradual shift from a darker tone to a lighter one or vice versa.

graphic arts. Printmaking, including etching, engraving, lithography, and other techniques for producing multiple copies of a picture.

grid sketch. A box containing evenly spaced horizontal and vertical lines that is used when making a copy of a drawing.

harmonize. Setting down colors so that none clashes with the others.

Impressionism. An art movement that originated in France in the late nineteenth century. Among the Impressionist painters are Paul Cezanne, Edouard Manet, and Claude Monet.

kaolin. A fine, white clay that is mixed with pigments to make the "lead" of colored pencils. Kaolin is also used to make porcelain.

optical mix. The effect achieved by superimposing layers of two (or more) colors that are blended by the eyes of the viewer to produce a third color.

outline. A quick sketch that with a few lines sets down the basic elements of a subject.

pigment. A colored powder obtained from earth, finely ground stones, vegetables, chemicals, etc., and mixed with a medium such as oil to make paints, with wax to make crayons, or with wax and clay to make colored pencils.

primary colors. Red, blue, and yellow; the colors that are blended to produce other colors, but that cannot themselves be obtained by any mixtures.

scale. A group of all the tone variations in a color.

secondary colors. Orange, purple, and green; the colors obtained by blending pairs of primary colors.

shading. Capturing light and shadows through gradation of different tones.

sketch. A rough drawing or painting in which the shape, composition, and tonal values of light and shadows are determined.

still life. A drawing or painting based on a collection of objects posed in a particular way by the artist.

tempera. A technique of painting in which the pigments are mixed in an egg white or egg yolk medium (rather than in oil). Tempera painting colors are less apt to change or crack than oil paintings.

tertiary colors. The colors obtained by blending a primary and secondary color (example, blue-green or red-orange.)

tone. Intensities of a color, from the lightest to the darkest.

transparent color. A layer of color through which the color underneath can be seen.

value. The degree of lightness or darkness of a color. A weak value is very light (or pale); a strong value is dark and intense.

warm colors. Those that in the color wheel are located between crimson and light yellow, with both these colors included.

Index